GIANTS AND DEMONS

Tadaka the Evil Demoness

SHUBHA VILAS

Om Books International

Lord Brahma had once blessed Yaksha King Suketu that the daughter that would be born to him would have the strength of a thousand elephants. That is how strong Tadaka, his daughter, turned out to be. She later gave birth to two robust demon sons Maricha and Subahu from her demon husband, Sunda.

Sunda loved to trouble and irritate the peaceful hermits in the forest while they performed their meditations and yagyas. But what he failed to realise was that the hermits, although fragile looking, had super powers. Especially Sage Agastya, whom he had targeted. Sage Agastya was so angry with him that he reduced the demon Sunda to ashes.

Tadaka, Maricha and Subahu, furious upon hearing the news of Sunda's death, became vengeful and pledged to destroy Agastya's hermitage. Tadaka turned her wrath upon the forests that were home to Agastya and the other sages, and annihilated the Malada and Karusa forests.

Her intense rage converted the once picturesque forests into deserted, thorny woodlands and she soon filled them with demons who constantly harassed the sages to chase them away.

The two forests were absolutely dry and deserted when Sage Vishwamitra brought Shri Rama and Laxman to those forests. Vishwamitra told them all about the evil and wicked deeds of Tadaka.

Rama held his bow with one hand, and pulled back the string with the other. The twang of the bow was so powerful that it shook the entire forest. The thunderous sound forced the birds to fly out of every tree for fear that the forest would be destroyed.

At the far end of the forest, the monstrous Tadaka was relaxing in a cave. She too heard the loud twang of the bow string. She found the thunderous sound of Rama's bow unbearable. In a rage, she ran out of her cave towards the source of the sound. She wanted to kill the one who had caused her such torment.

Rama and Lakshmana saw Tadaka running towards them from a distance. Her ghastly and monstrous features were becoming clearer as she inched closer. She was a giant with shoulders as strong as the Mandara Mountains, feet so huge and heavy that her footsteps left behind a trail of lakes.

She wore golden bangles, elephant head-studded earrings and a blood-oozing garland of elephants strung tail to trunk. Her teeth were like the trident of Yama, the god of death. Tadaka inched closer to Rama. Trapped under each of her footsteps were hundreds of living creatures.

Tadaka made herself invisible and began to hurl stones from different directions. She laughed out loud at Rama's plight. But she soon realised her fatal mistake. Rama immediately knew where she was and released an arrow towards the source of the sound.

The arrow pierced through her heart and tore out of her back and flew into the sky. Tadaka was dead. In an instant, her monstrous body fell to the ground.

The demigods, led by Indra, assembled and applauded Rama for killing the wicked demoness. They showered flowers on the brothers from the heavenly skies.